LEADERSHIP
REFLECTIONS

LEADERSHIP REFLECTIONS

52 LEADERSHIP PRACTICES IN THE AGE OF WORRY

Dr. Lisa M. Aldisert

ISBN: 1499586256
ISBN-13: 9781499586251
Library of Congress Control Number: 2015917199
CreateSpace Independent Publishing Platform
North Charleston, South Carolina

Other Works by Lisa Aldisert

Valuing People – How Human Capital Can be Your Strongest Asset

The Small Business Money Guide – How to Get It, Use It, Keep It
(co-authored with Terri Lonier)

Introduction

In 2009, I launched an e-zine, *Executive Insight Tip of the Week*, which is published weekly on Thursday. The concept is to provide a short vignette based on a specific leadership insight inspired by observations in the workplace. Each essay can be read in a couple of minutes and is designed to provide a tip the reader can apply on the job.

I have never lacked for things to write about because my work as an executive advisor provides me with an abundance of observations, examples, and anecdotes my subscribers can relate to. Having written hundreds of issues, I've accumulated a large body of content, and this volume contains fifty-two of these short essays in this volume.

Although the book can be scanned in about an hour, you can also focus on one topic each week. I've added a couple of questions at the end of each vignette so that you can reflect on your leadership or managerial skills. When you take a few minutes to reflect, it will give you fresh insights, sharpen your self-awareness, and, over time, build your confidence as a leader.

Leadership is a complex topic, one that has a multitude of interpretations, and is misunderstood by many. From my viewpoint, leadership starts with an attitude. A leader is someone who takes charge—sometimes overtly, other times less so—to move people, processes, or projects to a successful conclusion. You can be a leader without having a title people usually associate with leadership. You are a leader by your actions, not your position.

I'm particularly passionate about leaders who have an entrerpreneurial mindset. These individuals have character. They are original thinkers. They are superb communicators and demand the same from their people. They trust their guts. And they solemnly respect time, conscious that once it flees, it's gone.

Managers carry out the vision of leaders. The good ones are aligned with the leader's strategy and goals. The line between leader and manager is often blurred in today's workplace.

I think of the leader as the one who takes the plunge to make things happen and the manager as the one who executes. Importantly, sometimes they are the same person, especially in organizations that operate with lean organizational structures.

Leadership takes work. With so many variables and complexities, I find that many leaders fall into the trap of worrying about things they have no control over. This can take on a life of its own, so it's important to stay out of this trap.

In reading these vignettes over the years, many of my clients assumed I was writing about them or their staff. They sent me e-mails asking if I was writing about a particular incident of theirs. Sometimes yes, sometimes no.

Truth be told, each vignette is inspired by a "live event" but is written for universal appeal. If you see your employees (or yourself!) as you read, be comforted to know you are participating in that timeless parade of events in the workplace that makes us both jubilant and crazy.

I hope this volume gives you some ideas, makes you smile, and inspires you to higher leadership heights—maybe even some fearless leadership of your own.

And I invite you to sign up for *Executive Insight* at www.lisaaldisert.com. It's free, and you can unsubscribe at any time (which, of course, I hope you don't).

—*LMA*

CHAPTER 1

YOUR PEOPLE ARE WATCHING YOU

S ometimes you just don't know when your leadership makes a huge difference for someone. I witnessed this with a young colleague, who was sharing a story about something she had done with her team.

When I asked her if she realized the huge impact of her action, it was clear that she hadn't thought about it at all. Although she was genuinely pleased, it almost seemed like the surprise effect was more thrilling than what she had actually done.

You may not think about it, but your people are watching you. You never know when even the most obscure action or comment forms an impression.

Of course, this happens with both the good and the bad. When you become a leader, whether in an official capacity or not, you have to be mindful that people take their lead from what you do and how you do it.

Once I worked with someone whose bad behavior rippled throughout his firm. His managers realized that ignoring the situation and failing to intervene contributed to the problem, but they also wanted to salvage his employment. (*Hint*: When you have a toxic employee, it doesn't matter how good he or she is. It's almost always more work than it's worth.)

What I remember vividly from this engagement was this employee's complete unwillingness to change his behavior. He considered himself to be a "passionate person," and why should he temper that zeal in the workplace?

This person clearly had major emotional-intelligence issues, but by ignoring it for as long as they did, his leaders were, *de facto*, approving his demeanor, and the rest of the staff was influenced adversely.

Your people take their lead from your actions and behavior. Ignoring a situation can have as great an impact as celebrating a job well done.

For reflection:

- How do your leadership decisions impact your employees?
- Do you put your head in the sand by ignoring the impact of toxic employees?

CHAPTER 2

MANAGING WHEN YOU'RE "TOO BUSY"

D o you know leaders who think managing their people is a side job that interferes with their "real work"? Or those who become impatient because a team member needs help at "inconvenient" times? Or managers who become irritated because their staff didn't telepathically understand what they *really* wanted?

(Feel free to look in the mirror, by the way!)

When you answer "yes" to these kinds of questions, you may be suffering from too much work, feeling stressed about not fulfilling your goals, or frustrated with the entire idea of managing.

Here's the challenge: when you're a leader, people look to you for direction. There's no way around this, so you need to get used to it. If you're a manager, you need to deal with your staff whether you like it or not, have the time or not, and have the patience or not.

Many frustrated managers have the impression that "managing" is some ethereal, mysterious, foreign activity that they aren't good at executing. You may think that's the case, but it doesn't have to be.

Strange as it may seem, your staff most likely understands and appreciates the fact that you're overworked and stressed from accomplishing massive quantities of work in short periods of time (as they're in the same boat).

It doesn't require much to let your team know that you're on top of what they're doing *and* interested in their well-being.

Walk around a couple of times a day to check in with people.

If someone wants to talk to you when you're in the middle of something intense, ask if you can follow up with him or her at a certain time (and make sure you do so).

When someone needs help that will take more than a few minutes, schedule time to meet.

Catch people doing something right and acknowledge it, publicly when appropriate.

After completing a big initiative, take time to celebrate with the team.

For reflection:

- What annoys you about managing people, and when does this happen?
- What can you do to diffuse this annoyance?

CHAPTER 3

THE DANGER OF SETTLING

D o you settle for less? It doesn't matter what you settle for or when you do it...it can begin a pattern where your expectations and standards slip, and you're not even aware that it's happening.

This can be debilitating when it happens on the job. I know managers who will say, "Just this time," and before they know it, they're doing it all of the time.

When you settle, you create a major roadblock to excellence and high achievement. It sets a bad example for your staff, and over time, morale can slip and negativity can creep into the environment.

Settling can downsize your future before it has a chance to get started.

How can you prevent settling? First, be aware of what provokes it. Know your triggers, and prepare to combat them when they surface. Often people succumb to settling when they are tired, overwhelmed, or feeling particularly impatient, so think about what prompts you to do so.

Second, remember your "why." Why is it important for you to strive for excellence in a particular situation rather than settling? When you have clarity about why, it's easier to prevent settling from happening.

Next, project and reinforce an attitude of excellence. This acts as an antidote to settling. By consciously focusing on excellence, you diminish factors that get in the way.

No one likes to think that they settle for less, so remember that its impact multiplies when you're the leader and your people mimic your behavior. If you tend to settle, follow these suggestions, reverse the impact, and get back on the track of greater success.

For reflection:

- How can you avoid the danger of settling for less?
- What small things can you add to the work environment that promote excellence and achievement?

CHAPTER 4

STRIVE FOR EXCELLENCE, NOT PERFECTION

I'm fortunate to know many people who are driven to do their best all the time, every day, and in every circumstance. And when their performance is slightly off, they evaluate what didn't work, why it didn't work, and what could have been done differently.

Normally, this is a fabulous personal trait. It reflects a person who is responsible and accountable and who strives to be the best.

When the pursuit of excellence goes into overdrive, however, it may become detrimental to performance. An overfocus on what went wrong in the past can detract from moving forward. And an obsession with perfection in the future can cause significant stress that hinders results.

It's important to understand the distinction between excellence and perfection. Excellence implies superiority in the performance of an action, whereas perfectionism is the refusal to accept anything less than the gold standard.

When you focus on excellence and follow the tried-and-true process that works best for *you* (not your colleague, not your best friend, not your brother), the results will come.

It's worth taking the time to reflect on what excellence means to you, then consistently apply it to your process, whether it is sales, marketing, production, client service, or something else.

Here's a definition of excellence that can guide you:

- The state or fact of excelling; the possession chiefly of good qualities in an eminent or unusual degree; surpassing merit, skill, virtue, worth, etc.; dignity, eminence.
- Refusal to accept any standard short of perfection.
- To be superior or preeminent in the possession of some quality or in the performance of some action, usually in a good sense; to surpass others.

The bottom line is this: focus on your desired outcome, which is an excellent result, not a perfect one.

For reflection:

- How can you avoid the perfectionist trap?
- Consider the abovementioned definition of excellence. Pick what resonates most for you, and apply it on the job.

CHAPTER 5

LEADERSHIP DECISIVENESS

As a leader, you're always "on," whether you want to be or not (and whether you think about it or not). Your people, your clients, and your colleagues see it all. If you're revealing the good, the bad, and the ugly, you're headed for trouble.

People want to see confidence, decisiveness, and consistency in their leaders—don't you agree?

If you have a personality where you want people to like you, you really need to pay attention to your behavior when it comes to decision making.

First, you need to be clear that your decision is the best for your organization, regardless of size or circumstances. If you don't believe that you're making the best decision, people will know, and they will think (consciously or subconsciously) that you're weak.

Second, you can't make decisions based on popularity. People may not like your decisions, but if you're clear and confident, your people will give you the benefit of the doubt.

If you act with timidity, they're going to be all over you trying to change your mind. And if you let that happen, you're on your way to losing your presence as a leader.

Third, obviously you don't want to be rigid, but after you make a decision, you need to live with it. If you keep rethinking it, you'll make yourself crazy. You can always course-correct as you move ahead.

Finally, don't be so fearful in making a decision that you end up paralyzed. Your people will see that, too, and they will begin to take action randomly based on what they feel is appropriate.

The best way to become good at decision making is to do it. Don't procrastinate. Don't worry. Don't analyze it to death. Just do it.

For reflection:

- Identify areas where you can improve and enhance your decision-making skills.
- What prevents you from making decisions when you're stuck?

CHAPTER 6

ARE YOU AFRAID OF YOUR STAFF?

When I facilitate workshops on leadership, participants often ask questions about managing people. A common theme across these questions is their timidity as managers.

One example was an employee who was frequently absent under the auspices of FMLA (Family and Medical Leave Act). The employee is entitled to the time off but gives little notice each time, resulting in lack of coverage in the department. Who ends up covering? The manager.

Other examples relate to employee entitlement and how these managers could more effectively deal with employees' self-declared privileges.

One of my favorites, from a senior person in a high-tech company, was how to handle employees who said they couldn't attend a midafternoon new-product strategy meeting because they had an appointment to go mountain climbing!

In all these cases, it's up to the manager to set the tone and the ground rules of how things work in the office. If you don't do this, your staff will steamroll you and create their own ground rules.

When you establish expectations, you are defining an organizational culture. For example, when you ask that employees provide reasonable notice when requesting time off, this results in a culture of courtesy and professionalism. Expectations of employee accountability can strive to offset a mentality of entitlement.

This defines leadership. If you don't establish expectations around professional decorum and responsibility, the outcome will be up for grabs.

No one wants to admit to being afraid of their employees. But truth be told, if you're reticent to articulate your professional expectations, you aren't leading.

For reflection:

- What do your employees do that make you want to hide?
- How can you use humor to deflect some of these situations?

CHAPTER 7

WHAT HAPPENS WITH YOUR WANDERING MIND

Research reported in *Science* tracked how people feel during everyday situations using an iPhone app called trackyourhappiness.

One of the outcomes reported was that people tend to be happier when they focus on the activity that they're doing in the moment rather than thinking about something else. "In fact, whether and where their minds wandered was a better predictor of happiness than what they were doing," according to the results.

The researchers indicated that overall our minds wander some 47 percent of the time. Wow! Just think about what that means in the workplace. (If you think this percentage is low, we should talk!)

If your people are stimulated and engaged, chances are good they're more focused on their work. But imagine what's happening with those who are bored or frustrated or generally distracted.

As leaders, it reinforces the point that we need to stay focused, because that 47 percent statistic about wandering minds applies to everyone.

In case you think this doesn't apply to you, just think about how you respond to interruptions, what with e-mail, cell phones, texting, IM'ing…you get the picture. Eliminating distractions directly improves our focus, so it's up to us to manage ourselves and the disruptions that we face every day.

It doesn't matter whether we're happy or sad, energetic or sluggish, intentionally focused or deliberately daydreaming. A wandering mind is an equal-opportunity intrusion.

Give this some thought…after you turn off your phone.

For reflection:

- What's your best guess of what percentage of time your mind wanders?
- Think about the leadership implications of your answer.

CHAPTER 8

ARE YOU PAYING ATTENTION?

I had dinner with my friend, Deb, who was visitng in New York from out of town. We first knew each other professionally, had a strong initial connection, and became friends since then.

I told her how something she accomplished inspired a big decision that I made. She seemed genuinely surprised that her actions had influenced me.

This happens all of the time. You never know when something you say or do will resonate with someone and have an impact.

Think about how you gather information when you make a decision. You draw on information and resources that give you the insights and knowledge to decide effectively.

Sometimes a visible, public persona inspires us. More often than not, though, inspiration comes from the unexpected through the ordinary conversations and experiences in life.

But what are you missing if you're not paying attention?

Obviously, you'll miss something. You don't even know what you're going to miss, because you're simply not paying attention—imagine that!

Listening and observing are great skills to develop. Most people aren't very good at them, but it only takes a little discipline to cultivate and improve them.

Make a commitment to listen and observe a little more closely. What you see and hear may amaze and inspire you in the most unexpected way.

For reflection:

- Listen more attentively for the next week, and identify something that you may have otherwise missed.
- How can you pay more attention to your colleagues so that you "catch" a moment of inspiration?

CHAPTER 9

THE AVOCATIONAL LEADER

D o you ever think about the masks people wear? We all masquerade from time to time: we want to appear happy when we're miserable, interested when we're bored, enthusiastic when we're apathetic.

Recently I've become acquainted with a person—let's call him Sam—who created a strategic alliance with a group of independent practitioners. The idea has potential: strategic alliances make sense when the business case works and all who are involved profit from the association.

In this case, however, the leadership is missing. Well-intentioned as he is, Sam only occasionally engages in this endeavor, and as a result, the practitioners are clueless about everything from the business model to what is expected of them. He treats the business as a hobby, hence the "avocational leader."

In thinking about Sam, I realize that many people do this. Leadership is an afterthought. Instead of being true leaders, they only sporadically don leadership masks.

Being a leader takes work. I'm not saying it has to be hard, but you need to focus on it. You can't just do it when your schedule eases up or you have a few minutes to call the office from the airport.

Weak or inadequate leadership trickles down to your people. They aren't going to give you tips to become better at it; instead, they're going to do their own thing and disregard you as a leader.

Of course, I'm not writing about you…but just in case… take a look in the mirror, and make sure that you're not just wearing a mask and only occasionally acting the part.

For reflection:

- When do you hide behind a mask as a leader?
- How can you become more proactive when you just aren't interested?

CHAPTER 10

MANAGING HIGH-PERFORMING TALENT

S arah is a highly talented, aggressive professional working in a boutique investment bank. Her new manager, Sean, is pulling out his hair because Sarah is *so* independent, and quite frankly, she isn't particularly interested in being managed by Sean.

He wants her to write reports; she wants to do deals. He wants her to track her time; she can't imagine *wasting* her time by tracking it. He wants her to introduce him to all of her clients; she sees no value in this.

Welcome to the world of the top performer. Managers like Sean are in a no-win situation when they apply old-school managerial tactics to highly talented top performers.

I know some of you may be bristling. Who does she think she is by responding to her manager in such a way? If this thought crossed your mind, then there is a 99.9 percent chance that you're still using old-school managerial tactics as well.

It's time to move on.

Don't manage top performers by putting a noose around their necks. Instead, respectfully support their efforts and see *what you can do for them* so that they crank out more revenue-generating, high-margin work for your firm. For example, Sean can appeal to Sarah's strengths by brainstorming ideas related to deals. Here are a few additional thoughts:

- *Don't choke them with rules and procedures.* They'll rebel in nine cases out of ten, so save yourself the exasperation.
- *Ask open-ended questions.* You'll learn more about how they think and feel, and this will give you more insight into how to manage them.
- *Give them space to be creative.* They don't like feeling bureaucratic or ordinary.

I know a lot of managers who were effective using command and control techniques in past corporate jobs. Overall, it's a losing proposition today, and even more dramatically so when you have a team of high performers.

For reflection:

- What can you do to add value to your top performers?
- What's the best way to manage them without cramping their style?

CHAPTER 11

MANAGEMENT MYOPIA

Have you ever faced a situation where you've clung to an old "story" about an employee even if the circumstances have changed? For example, let's say you reigned in a "renegade" employee six months ago, and the person subsequently adjusted to the way *you* want him to behave.

Now the former scenario no longer exists. And you've recently discovered that the employee is underperforming because he's following your previous directives to the letter and ignores taking advantage of new opportunities.

You don't want to loosen your grip over him, though, because you still believe he could revert to his old behavior. From your perspective, "He'll still be out of control" or "I don't want the management headache."

This is management myopia.

The easy thing to do is to do nothing. After all, you already assessed the situation, and the person has abided by the status quo. He's "under control."

The harder action is to take a fresh look, evaluate what has changed, and determine how the person's skills and talents can now be best utilized.

It's a dangerous management practice to pigeonhole employees based on the old stories. Using this example, if the person was really a renegade, he would have continued on that path regardless of your warnings.

By doing nothing, you're not managing. And if you do this with one person, who knows what other opportunities are being lost because of your inaction?

The more spirited the employee, the harder he or she is to manage. But the upside is also probably greater. If you're not willing to do your job and manage, maybe you're in the wrong job.

Open your eyes and make sure you're seeing truth rather than fiction. You may be surprised at what doors open next.

For reflection:

- When does management myopia kick in for you?
- What are some ways that you can manage "spirited" employees more effectively?

CHAPTER 12

DO YOUR EMPLOYEES ENHANCE OR DETRACT?

You know the sound you make with a straw when your drink is almost finished? Think of that as the sound of people who work for you who just go through the motions. They are sucking productivity right out from under you.

If you haven't done so recently, you'd be well served to see which of your people are really working and which are more or less taking up space.

I came across a great example of this when I was trying to get transportation from the airport on a recent trip. The person who was supposed to help customers was especially ineffective (my euphemism for "a complete waste of time").

He spent most of our conversation disparaging his company: how unreliable they were, how they constantly upset their customers, how they did a terrible job. Not coincidentally, he was the poster guy for someone you'd never want to work for you.

This was in contrast to the person who actually took me to my destination. She was engaging and pleasant: personable, professional, and cheerful.

The guy at the airport devalues her and her colleagues' good work because he's just going through the motions. His ailment goes beyond presenteeism (a situation when employees show up for work and only pretend to work). Had I not had many prior positive experiences with this company, I might have easily walked away and selected another option.

Do your employees enhance or detract from the mission of your business? Be scrupulously honest with yourself. I know leaders who turn the other cheek, largely for irrational reasons, and that begins the loud sucking noise I mentioned at the beginning.

Pay attention, and more importantly, take action with those who aren't doing their jobs. This isn't always an easy task, but you're in charge, and it's up to you to make it work the way it's supposed to work.

For reflection:

- Do a quick scan of your employees, and identify those who enhance and those who detract.
- What actions can you take to change or eliminate the detractors?

CHAPTER 13

THE DICHOTOMY OF A BELOVED EMPLOYEE

One of my friends is the managing partner of a busy medical practice with several doctors, a variety of specialized employees, and an often-hectic reception area. One of his employees has been a front-desk icon to the patients.

This person, who I'll call Greg, is the epitome of client service. He is exactly the kind of employee who makes a medical practice shine, especially during times of stress. He is warm, compassionate, and efficient, and he always has a good sense of humor.

You know a "but" is coming. As good a medical receptionist, patient wrangler, and soother of frayed nerves as Greg is, he's unfortunately a lousy employee.

After years of working in this job, he began to set his own rules, which changed based on the circumstances and his mood. Sadly, he became difficult to work with.

And, regrettably, Greg no longer works there.

The reason something like this happens (especially in a hectic client-facing environment) is that someone isn't managing. Greg couldn't be great at client service—and work there for ten years—if he hadn't started as a good employee.

What happened was that he gradually started to do what *he* wanted to do, which interfered with and detracted from how others did their jobs.

It's hard to pinpoint when something like this starts. You don't easily see the negative with beloved employees (after all, how many employees can you call "beloved"?). It creeps up on you so that one day you look at the person and wonder how you ever hired him or her in the first place.

You can't be afraid to proactively manage a favored employee, especially if you're worried about hurt feelings or, even worse, the fear that the person will leave as a result of your tough love. If you let it get out of hand, the person is going to leave anyway, based on *your* decision.

Manage your favorites with the same standards you use for all your employees. Some days it won't be easy or pleasant, but overall, you'll cut off a bad situation before it gets out of hand.

For reflection:

- Identify any favored employees, and evaluate how you manage them.
- How can you manage these employees more effectively?

CHAPTER 14

WHY CAN'T MORE EMPLOYEES BE LIKE JOSE?

I meet with a client once a month or so over breakfast. One of the servers at the restaurant, Jose, is so good at his job that I find myself wondering how more employees could have his amazing work ethic.

Jose is always one step ahead. He doesn't know us by name, but he recognizes us, greets us, and treats us as if we had breakfast there every day. The little extras (one of my favorites being coffee in a fresh cup after the meal) make the experience special.

He has worked there for over twenty years and shared that he enjoys his work because of his interactions with customers and coworkers. He feels valued by management, and of course, the impact of that can't be underestimated.

Contrast this to the employee who is chronically late to work; to the one who calls in sick at every opportunity; to the one who is ready at 4:15 to bolt out of the office at 5:00; to the one who puts in minimal effort and doesn't care about the output; to the one who is always right and never accountable when something goes wrong.

Strong work ethic isn't dead; we just don't pay enough attention to it when we hire and manage people. I speak for most of my colleagues and clients when I say that it's better to hire someone who has a good work ethic and average skills than someone with good skills and a horrible attitude about work.

You can train for skills, but it's hard to manage someone who is doing you a big favor showing up at work every day.

Think about what "strong work ethic" means in your organization and identify the three to five most important characteristics that are relevant for you. Make this the foundation of your expectations, and be relentless about communicating what this means and upholding this standard.

Remember, it's up to you to lead the way. Make a strong work ethic an imperative, and you'll see a different quality of results. The ones who follow your lead will surprise you, and the ones who don't will fall by the wayside.

For reflection:

- Evaluate the work ethic of your staff, and identify the pluses and minuses.
- How can you better assess work ethic during the hiring process?

CHAPTER 15

"LOVE THE ONE YOU'RE WITH"

The topic of love in the workplace may seem a little unusual, but when you think about it, most weeks we're with our colleagues for more hours than we spend with our families. If you don't at least *like* the people you work with, it can create an unpleasant and sometimes even disagreeable work environment.

This comes to mind frequently when I'm working with clients whose team members don't communicate effectively or don't play well in the sandbox. It makes me wonder how people can be in close quarters, day in and day out, and not respect each other enough to at least show a little "like."

I often say people don't need to become best friends with their coworkers, but if they really don't like each other, they should seriously question whether the job is worth it. After all, if you don't "like the ones you're with," discomfort and stress may be just around the corner.

Leaders need to be mindful of this. Don't assume everyone likes each other. In fact, many times, you won't even know that issues exist until something bubbles up and erupts. If you find out about it then, it takes a lot more work to repair the damage and eliminate any residual bad feelings.

Take your cues from the nonverbal, as it's unlikely people will blurt out negative opinions of their coworkers to the boss. Also, you'll learn something if someone repeatedly refers to a coworker in a sarcastic tone.

Take time to see whether your folks are at least "in like." You'll be glad you checked.

For reflection:

- How can you best observe to see the degree to which "like" happens in your team dynamics?
- How do you handle employees whose mutual dislike of each other detracts from results?

CHAPTER 16

LOCATION DISLOCATION

Have you ever noticed how many people exhibit behavior in public places that is best left for more private venues? You may not think about this explicitly, but consider these examples:

- The disgruntled employee who sets up a lunchtime appointment for career-management advice and tells the consultant that he'll have trouble getting cell-phone reception in his company cafeteria.
- The lawyer who discusses confidential information on his cell phone on a commuter train.
- The foursome in a restaurant whose loud and obnoxious behavior distracts everyone sitting at surrounding tables.
- The person who discusses private information about a coworker on an elevator.
- The doctor who reprimands staff in front of patients or their family members.

I'm sure you have examples to add to this list. The theme of "location dislocation" is inappropriate behavior in public, but it is symptomatic of lack of judgment. When people consistently act improperly in public places, chances are they lack judgment in other areas.

Managers need to be mindful of these slips, because even unintentionally, these slips can show up in business settings, resulting in negative consequences.

Coaching someone who has bad judgment is a long-term proposition, and the first step is to make the person aware of what he or she is doing and why it can have a detrimental outcome.

It may be awkward to discuss, but the potential damage by doing nothing is worse than the discomfort of having the conversation.

Pay attention to location dislocation in your workplace. The awareness that comes from observing will heighten your managerial perspective.

For reflection:

- What can you do to eliminate "location dislocation" in your office?
- How do you address the issue of judgement from someone who seems to have none?

CHAPTER 17

DO YOU HAVE "LONE RANGER" LEADERS?

I've worked with a leadership team where three out of four people are aligned around organizational goals, while the fourth is singing to the tune of his own agenda (which has been determined to be *not* in the best interests of the company).

This leader is valued in his role, but if he doesn't align with his colleagues, over time it will infect the leadership team. Although the CEO is reluctant to deal with this, my advice is to deal with it immediately.

The longer a lone ranger marches to the beat of a different drum, the longer it will take to reel him or her back.

You don't want to confront a lone ranger with threats; rather, you want to point out why his or her behavior can derail the company's goals. As talented as the person might be, if he or she doesn't get on board, it's best to think about alternatives.

This CEO wants to discover *why* the lone ranger is off on his own path. This is a noble approach, but the bottom line is that trying to figure out "why" may take a long time, and it will most likely continue disrupting the other leaders.

When a team aligns, the results are far superior to when it operates disparately. Think of any high-functioning sports team as an analogy.

Lone-ranger leaders are often people who were super-talented in an area of specialization before they moved into leadership roles. A great salesperson, for example, has competencies to bring in new business, but not necessarily the skills to manage and develop other salespeople.

If you have a situation like this, it's best to nip it in the bud before it spins out of control. An aligned leadership team can accomplish so much more in a short period of time than a team limping along because one person is a rugged individualist.

For reflection:

- How do you maintain individuality among leaders while aligning around organizational goals?
- How can you engage your leadership team to align around values?

CHAPTER 18

STAND UP AND CHEER

Many leaders in the workplace don't practice the art of recognition. Whether they don't think it's important or they simply forget about it, they don't acknowledge the good work their staff or coworkers perform on a routine basis.

The sad truth is that thousands of employees go to work every day tainted with low-grade depression because they don't feel valued by their leaders. The good news is that this is easy to fix, and it doesn't cost you any time or money.

This pops up as a recurring theme among my clients. Even executive-level professionals feel unappreciated.

Recognition is important for morale, and denying your people a moment of acknowledgment can diminish your stature as a leader.

I'm not suggesting you dispense false praise or insincere flattery. That will immediately resonate as phony and will backfire if you attempt it.

You can recognize the little things, however, and this will make a big difference in the attitude of your staff. Here are some simple examples:

"Thanks for working late to finish that report."

"The design of the PowerPoint really enhanced the content."

"Joe appreciated the time you took to explain the background of the problem."

"I never thought of that—thanks for the suggestion."

"Scheduling everyone on one day made everything easier for the team."

Many times, cranky behavior can be eliminated by small boosters like these. The bottom line is that people want to know they are valued for the work that they do.

For reflection:

- What can you do to stand up and cheer for your staff?
- How do you think this will affect them?

CHAPTER 19

THE FEEDBACK IMPERATIVE

Does your team have clearly defined roles, responsibilities, and expectations for performance? If it doesn't, it can be a recipe for trouble. Think about it: if people don't have clarity about what they're supposed to do and how they'll be evaluated, they'll walk around in the dark.

Consider these examples:

- A client-relationship manager doesn't understand the full scope of what her job entails, and as a result, clients do not feel they are being served properly. Her supervisor, who is frustrated by clients' complaints, doesn't give her proper feedback, which means the same mistakes occur over and over again.

- A senior manager walks into a contentious situation in his company, doesn't understand the politics, and proceeds to provoke other members of the management team. His leader avoids giving feedback, so this manager continues to irritate his colleagues and loses effectiveness in getting things done.

- A manager ignores the problems caused by a disgruntled team member who creates a toxic work environment. His managerial style is to ignore the situation and hope that it goes away.

When I've raised questions about these and similar scenarios, often the answer is "they should know better."

Although that may be the case, when you don't provide feedback, it's almost as if you expect them to be clairvoyant. It's your job as the leader to tell your people what they're doing (right *and* wrong) and to give them the tools and resources to improve where shortfalls occur.

Avoid the clairvoyance trap and take action. It isn't always easy to provide constructive feedback, but developing this skill will make a difference, not just with the person involved but with the team as a whole.

For reflection:

- How can you more proactively deliver feedback to your team?
- How can you improve the way in which you provide feedback?

CHAPTER 20

MASTERING THE ART OF FEEDBACK

M any managers struggle with how to give feedback to their employees, and as a result they aren't successful in conveying what they really want to say. As a result, delivering feedback can be one of the more stressful parts of their job.

At one end of the spectrum are managers who are so brutally blunt that the sting of their harsh words is more powerful than the underlying message. At the other end are managers who couch their feedback in positive and flowery comments so that their employees completely miss the message.

You want to land somewhere in the middle: deliver your message clearly and effectively without wounding the person receiving the feedback.

Giving feedback takes practice. Here are some tips to improve your skills, particularly when feedback is sensitive.

Be clear on your ultimate message. Is the person missing deadlines? Ignoring important details? Annoying coworkers? Go to the heart of the issue first, and then figure out how to say it.

Rehearse. Write down the main points to support your message. Practice saying these points with the goal of expressing yourself naturally and confidently. You might find that you're way too wordy the first few times, for example, so experiment until you find the right words.

Use an example. People connect with stories, anecdotes, and examples. Craft an example that illustrates your point, and use it to augment the point itself.

Listen "between the lines." Give your employee the opportunity to comment, and proactively listen. Even if you disagree with what he or she says, a feedback session goes better when the person feels heard.

The underpinning of these tips is to gather, organize, and craft your thoughts first rather than spewing reactive comments. When you approach it this way, you'll feel calmer and more confident—and a lot less stressed out.

For reflection:

- When do you "trip over" giving feedback?
- How can you become more effective in delivering feedback?

CHAPTER 21

THE MAGICAL WORLD OF MANAGEMENT

I n his excellent book, *Good to Great*, Jim Collins talks about not only hiring great people but hiring the best people for specific jobs. His expression, "getting the right people on the bus," became one of the most memorable metaphors from the book.

I've observed that leaders hope new people will seamlessly start a new job, get up to speed, and perform up to expectations without knowing anything substantive about the new job, the new company, the corporate culture, and your actual expectations for performance.

In other words, they expect magic!

Even if you have a magic wand, in the magical world of management, *you* need to put in some work before the magic happens. When people complain about how their employees aren't doing their jobs, often it's because they don't give enough direction and guidance.

True enough, some of your people might not be the right ones on the bus, but before you think about throwing them off course, consider your role as manager and coach. What can you do differently that will result in a better outcome? Here are some ideas:

- Clarify your expectations so people know how they're supposed to do their jobs.
- Meet with your team as a group to share your vision for the coming year and show them how their work contributes to your vision.
- Meet individually so you can clearly understand their perspectives and challenges, and reinforce the connection between their jobs, organizational goals, and your expectations.
- Where mismatches occur, take action immediately to remedy them.
- Work with your people to realign them where appropriate.

These ideas can be a baseline to help you navigate the magical world of management. Just remember to take action.

For reflection:

- When do you fall into the trap of expecting magic?
- From the examples above, identify one way you can be more proactive.

CHAPTER 22

THERE IS NO SUCH THING AS TOO MUCH COMMUNICATION

Clear communication is one of the key management issues that people struggle with constantly. Even when you do it well, sometimes you need to repeat it, say it differently, or ask them to repeat it back in their words so that you know that you're on the same page.

It isn't that the entire world suffers from ADHD (even though sometimes it might seem that way); the basic ways that we read, write, speak, and listen have changed.

For example, like many people, you probably spend a lot of time in front of screens: computers, tablets, smartphones, even smart watches. People don't read on screen; they *scan.* And simply put, you don't get the same comprehension from scanning.

And when you're scanning, myriad other distractions enter the picture: interruptions from coworkers, phone calls, texts, instant messages. No wonder concentration suffers!

Someone misinterpreted my response to his e-mail ("OK—I'm good with this"). He read it to be the opposite of what I said. I apologized for not being clear (really?), and he conceded that he didn't pay attention as he skimmed through a hundred e-mails.

And that brings me back to the main point, which is to be critically mindful of how people receive your message—especially in this distraction-laden world. Even if you think you couldn't be clearer, don't assume that people heard you the way you intended and expected.

For reflection:

- Practice mindful listening: don't look at e-mail or documents when someone is talking to you.
- What techniques can you use to ensure that people understand what you're saying?

CHAPTER 23

Managing by telepathy

Continuing on the same theme as the previous essay, a recurring management theme is leaders who *assume* their people know what's on their minds. I call this "managing by telepathy," as these leaders often neglect to verbalize or e-mail what they want.

This is rarely intentional. After all, you don't sit in your office and think about how you can avoid good communication with your people. But you can get swept up in the busyness of your day and simply think that you said something, when it never left your mind.

Executives who complain about communication challenges are often guilty of weak communication skills themselves. When I drill down about exactly *how* they communicate, it doesn't take too long to discover that they "forget" to mention specific directives or details.

One way to keep your thoughts organized is to keep running lists for the various individuals or groups that you address on a regular basis. As an example, you can keep a running list for staff meetings, for key managers, or for specific projects. Then when you meet with them, you're not relying on memory or leaving a string of e-mails after the fact.

It doesn't matter what method you use to manage these lists; what is important is that you keep them. You can use a notebook, the tasks function in Outlook, and any number of programs or apps.

I know this may seem super obvious, but you know that the little things can make a big difference when it comes to communication.

I recommend that you not only try keeping person-specific running lists, but also observe how your communication improves as a result. At a minimum, your people will be relieved from the ongoing challenge of trying to read your mind.

For reflection:

- What organizational system works best for you?
- How can you expand this system to keep your outstanding items better organized?

CHAPTER 24

LEADING BY SOUND BITE

I was struck by an editorial Tom Friedman wrote for the *New York Times* on "The Rise of Popularism." He first heard the term while traveling in London. He comments, "It's the über-ideology of our day. Read the polls, track the blogs, tally the Twitter feeds and Facebook postings and go precisely where the people are, not where you think they need to go. If everyone is 'following,' who is leading?"

Extrapolating from this, how *do* you lead in 140 characters or less? If you spend time crafting a short blurb for the social-media kingdom, how do you remember the underlying concept? If you lead by sound bite, can you still convey conviction?

Of course, this has implications in the workplace. We already compete with people (employees and clients alike) pinging each other while they attend our presentations, demonstrations, and explanations.

(I even attended a court hearing as a witness for a client when the claimant was texting during the hearing. You can't make up these things!)

Those who spend the most time following and responding on social media have adapted to communicating in short bites.

The degree to which you experience this in your workplace depends on your corporate culture. It may be transparent, or you may rarely experience it.

One way or the other, it will catch up to you, so you need to learn how to distill important messages in succinct language.

I'm not suggesting that you lead by sound bite; I'm saying that there will be times when you'll want to be prepared. Otherwise, those who listen to you may create their own shortened versions that don't capture the essence that you want to convey.

It seems crazy to do this, but at least your annotated version will have a chance to embrace the core of your message. Remember, the synthesis of a concept is different from starting with an abbreviated idea.

I know that some of you will resist this idea. That's OK. Eventually you'll see it for yourself...perhaps on Twitter.

For reflection:

- How can you articulate your organizational mission in a few succinct, understandable sentences?
- How can you describe your expectations as a leader in a few brief sentences?

CHAPTER 25

THE VOICE OF A GROUP

I had the privilege of being a member of a group of twenty professionals participating in an adult learning forum. This forum was an immersion, and as such, we experienced a lot of togetherness.

Early on, two voices dominated the others, and although they expressed vastly different points of view, they had a similar impact on the rest of us.

First, their comments were more about themselves and their point of view than about the topic we were discussing. Second, they were oblivious that they weren't connecting with the rest of us. Third, they relentlessly tried to "sell" their ideas to us without regard to relevance.

This scenario happens in meetings everywhere, every week, in every imaginable venue.

Distractions arise when one or more voices dominate. Granted, this is a big topic, but here are a few ideas about how to develop the voice of a group that meets on a regular basis.

- Establish ground rules, or norms, about how the interaction and behavior of the group will occur. If you don't take the time to do this, the situation has the possibility to spiral out of control fairly quickly.
- If the group meets regularly about a specific project, clearly identify the roles of the members and the expectations around the individual contributions, time frames, and deliverables.
- When things don't go well, ensure that bad feelings don't fester. Establish a process in advance for how you will handle conflict.

This kind of group dynamic can be very powerful when appropriately managed. You will learn new ideas, test your beliefs, and see things through a different lens.

For reflection:

- How does your own voice contribute to group dynamics?
- How can you participate with groups without being either too dominating or too timid?

CHAPTER 26

TRANSCENDING BAD VIBES

A friend of mine is a senior leader in an organization that is undergoing tumultuous times. We've talked about the pain of keeping your team motivated when it's hard to go into the office every day.

This is about transcending negativity, ignoring bad publicity, and not dwelling on the feeling that the ship is rudderless.

If you're in this type of environment, here are some ways to maximize productivity and minimize pessimism and distractions.

It starts with attitude. Your people look to you for how to respond and what to do. They study every nuance, so your attitude and behavior trump the words that you say. If you focus on achieving results, they will follow suit. If you're morose and lethargic, their energy and initiative will drop.

Tell the truth. In many cases, the truth might be, "I really *don't* know what's going on." Honesty goes a long way to defray anxiety. If the news is bad, don't sugarcoat it. Be practical and pragmatic when you set the course for the weeks or months ahead.

Roll up your sleeves. Leading by example goes a long way at such times. Even more important, do what you can to eliminate the obstacles that your people face so they can do their jobs easier and better.

Connect with humor. Humor is an antidote to any gloomy environment. I'm not suggesting you act like Pollyanna, but when you inject appropriate humor, it breaks the overcast of gloom and lifts everyone's spirits.

Leave the office. Make sure everyone gets out one time during the day. Working straight through the day and eating lunch at your desk (if you even remember to do so) for weeks at a time isn't healthy. Even a ten-minute walk changes your mood and refreshes your perspective.

None of these ideas requires special technology, exceptional talent, or extra time. They take intention and sincerity, and they will make a difference.

For reflection:

- How do you stack up as a crisis manager?
- How can you improve for the benefit of your staff?

CHAPTER 27

WHAT WILL YOU GIVE UP?

I s there something you do, an aspect of your communication style, mannerisms, or idiosyncrasies, that doesn't serve you well in your leadership role?

This is especially important, since you model behavior your employees observe and often adopt as their own.

I once worked with two visible, top-performing leaders in a professional services firm. They ran a multiple-hundred-million-dollar practice and were renowned not only in their firm but globally in their industry.

In spite of their excellent results, they needed to "improve their interpersonal skills" (translation: *no one* got along with them). They had been so rude and abrasive to their staff that a senior-level employee filed a legal complaint against them.

Bottom line: they were terrorizing their team.

Neither of them thought that they were doing anything wrong, and in fact, neither understood why they were asked to work with me. The head of the group knew he was coarse and uncompromising, but he didn't care. He attributed his style to "cultural differences." He knew he was an outstanding practitioner in his field and felt this was what mattered.

Now here is the bizarre twist. It turned out the other leader *mimicked* the group head's style because she assumed this was the best way to be successful. Even though it felt uncomfortable, it had never occurred to her that harsh behavior was inappropriate.

When I asked her if she'd be willing to give up that behavior, she agreed to do so in a heartbeat. The group head was a little tougher, but he acquiesced when he considered the consequences of a lawsuit.

What might you give up? I doubt your weakness is as dramatic as the one in this example, but chances are, you can change something that will make you a more effective leader.

Think about teaming up with an accountability partner. Each of you can identify something you want to give up, and report back to each other regularly on your progress. Not only will this help you stay on task, but you and your partner can provide feedback to each other.

For reflection:

- Work on one thing at a time; pick the behavior or skill that will make the biggest difference when improved.
- What excuses do you use when you resist changing something that impedes your effectiveness?

CHAPTER 28

TRY A LIGHTER BALL

One of my clients hosted a bowling outing as a morale-building activity at her company. We were laughing about the experience of bowling, especially if you haven't bowled since your sixth-grade class went to Johnny's birthday bowling bash.

My client reported she didn't do very well in the first round, but then she improved by using a lighter ball.

Of course, when I heard this, I thought about how often we do things the "hard way" in the workplace, when using a "lighter ball" would make life so much easier.

Many managers make things much harder than they need to. They stress out over what to say, how to say it, what to do, the right timing…you get the idea.

What can you do to carry a lighter ball?

Delegate more. Yes, someone else will do something differently than you will, but effective coaching or guidelines will lead to the desired result. And it will reduce your to-do list.

Ask. Don't try to do everything alone. Speak with others who may have the knowledge or expertise to help you.

Take a break. Often, the ball gets heavier because we work nonstop without taking a break. Even a five-minute walk around the block (or your parking lot) can refresh perspective.

Make a phone call. Reach out to a client or colleague you haven't talked to recently. That conversation will trigger fresh perspective. (Yes, a phone call—not an e-mail or text!)

Seasonal or cyclical quirks of your business can result in the feeling of carrying a heavier ball from time to time. Keep these ideas in mind so you can stay agile when those periods arise.

For reflection:

- If you are challenged with delegating tasks, commit to delegate at least one task a day.
- Identify an activity you can do in a minibreak during the day to reenergize.

CHAPTER 29

MANAGERIAL SELF-PRESERVATION

One of the challenges in busy, growing organizations is how overwhelmed everyone gets. Pressure mounts as people try to keep up with the ever-increasing demands and burdens characteristic of a growth environment.

Of course, managers need to watch this. Mistakes happen. Nerves can be frayed. Anxiety builds. All these things contribute to a recipe for some pretty serious stress.

Managers especially need to pay attention to their own reactions in this environment. Often, as they attempt to support their teams, they dip into "doing the doing." This can start off small: a little task here, a deadline there.

But this becomes habit-forming, and the next thing you know, you're doing considerably more of the work than is expected of managers. More importantly, the business of managing doesn't get done.

What do you do in these situations?

First, gather your team and discuss your expectations during these high-demand periods. Everyone needs to know the importance of bearing their share of the load.

Next, monitor their progress, and assist by providing additional resources to the best of your ability.

Redistribute workloads. Some people may have capacity for more work, and it's entirely appropriate to engage them in additional work.

Diligently keep track of what needs to be accomplished so things don't fall through the cracks. These scenarios are ripe for what seems less important (but isn't) to disappear.

Take time for short breaks. These are necessary to stay sane during the insanity.

Managing overwhelming periods isn't easy, but it's an important skill for managers to master for their self-preservation.

For reflection:

- Think about where you get stuck and how you can prevent it from happening.
- Identify a trigger that prevents you from "doing the doing."

CHAPTER 30

MANAGERIAL BLIND SPOTS

Everyone has blind spots. You know what I mean—a relationship with someone where you are oblivious to flaws visibly annoying to anyone else in the universe. An example is the blind spots doting parents have on their badly behaving children who wreak havoc at the table next to you in a restaurant.

But blind spots can be devastating in the workplace, particularly if you're a leader.

If one of your employees has shortcomings everyone sees—except you—you could be headed for some serious trouble.

I know you're thinking you're smart enough that this could never happen to you, but believe me, you're wrong. (That's why they call it a *blind* spot...)

Often there is a correlation between a blind spot and a passionate desire to avoid conflict. In fact, that correlation is directly proportionate: the greater the desire to keep the peace, the bigger the blind spot.

So, what are your blind spots? Before you automatically respond, "I don't have any," think about these questions:

- Do you consistently brush off complaints about a particular employee?
- Have you (over) defended the behavior of a particular coworker or a decision you made?
- Do you change the subject when the same uncomfortable matter is raised?

If you're feeling uncomfortable reading this, then you may have a blind spot. If you do, you need to face it and take action.

For reflection:

- Do you ignore conflicts in order to keep peace?
- How can you alter your approach to be more effective?

CHAPTER 31

OVERCOMING YOUR BLIND SPOTS

The previous essay addressed the topic of managers who have blind spots about particular employees, why this is a problem, and how to determine if you have a blind spot.

The subject hit a nerve, because after it was published, many people e-mailed me with questions and comments!

So, now you know that you have blind spots…what are you going to do about it?

- *Listen carefully.* Objectively take in any feedback you may receive from employees about your blind spot. Don't react; just listen.
- *Analyze.* As you review the feedback, consider what makes you uncomfortable. Separate the elements of truth from otherwise illusive comments.

- *Evaluate.* Is this a situation that requires a conversation with the employee (who is the object of the blind spot), or do you simply need to change your behavior? If you need to have a conversation:
  - *Prepare.* Get comfortable with the facts that you can address.
  - *Script.* Write down the key points you want to address (don't leave this to memory).
  - *Cool off.* Approach the conversation objectively and unemotionally.
- *Intent.* In either case, ensure that your intent is to eliminate the blind spot to create a better working environment.

You know from other difficult situations that thinking about it is usually worse than actually doing it. Make a decision to face the challenge, prepare for it, and then take the action.

For reflection:

- What will you commit to do to overcome your blind spots?
- What is the benefit to you personally if you accomplish this?

CHAPTER 32

ARE YOU AS CHARMING AS A TRAFFIC COP?

*C*BS *Sunday Morning* once featured a story about Los Angeles sheriff's deputy Elton Simmons. Mr. Simmons had been a traffic cop on the force for over twenty years, and he bears the distinction of *never* having received any complaints during that time. Can you imagine issuing over twenty-five thousand tickets and receiving no flack?

The journalist who covered the story shadowed the deputy to see *how* he did his job. Some of the comments from people who received tickets ranged from "a great smile" to "a nice guy" to "disarming" to "never so happy to get a ticket."

The deputy had an easygoing demeanor and masterfully defused the stress that inevitably comes along when receiving a ticket. The journalist commented that Deputy Simmons had the "pitch-perfect mix of authority and diplomacy, with none of the attitude that sometimes comes with a cop."

This is a great example of inspiration from an everyday situation. If Deputy Simmons can create a positive experience out of receiving a traffic ticket, imagine what you—and your people—can do in the course of the workday.

Many employees are burdened by the reality of having less time to accomplish more with fewer resources. As a result, tensions can build when trying to meet deadlines.

People who handle these scenarios with a calm demeanor, similar to that of the deputy, not only keep themselves cool under pressure; they accomplish more and are much more agreeable to work with.

How do you translate this to the workplace? One idea might be to create a weekly contest where every day each team member writes a brief compliment about one colleague's positive demeanor that day. At the end of the week, the team can create an award for the person with the most positive comments.

This has the potential to get creative, and over time, the crankiest people on the team are going to feel pressure to change their ways.

Who knows? Maybe you will inspire a journalist to write about you!

For reflection:

- What do you think your team members would say about you?
- How do you get buy-in for an idea like this?

CHAPTER 33

SELF-SABOTAGE

Sometimes, smart people get in their own way and sabotage their potential success.

I've worked with someone who is focused on developing more assertiveness in her new leadership role. We've worked on various areas for improvement, including stronger communication skills.

One of her issues has been feeling that she is not "being heard" by her leadership team, and she has been frustrated about how to handle this. Of course, we've addressed this in some detail, including role-playing and scripting. Based on what she reported back to me, I thought her communication skills were improving.

Last week I observed her in a meeting and discovered that in spite of what she has reported back, her meandering, ponderous presentation style hasn't changed.

I gave her feedback after the meeting, suggesting her coworkers tune her out because she just doesn't get to the point. She confided that she just couldn't use a script in a "live" situation because it felt fake to her. Inertia has set in, and she's too afraid to try something that will take her out of her comfort zone.

When you commit to become a better leader, sometimes the things you try may feel awkward. This is part of the territory. When you commit to improving but resist the process, you're getting in your own way.

Bottom line: A coach provides guidance and direction, but the protégé needs to do the doing.

I invite you to take a moment of self-reflection to make sure you're not falling victim to self-sabotage. And if you are, it's time to get rid of it.

For reflection:

- Can you identify instances when you sabotage your efforts?
- What can you do to reverse the effects of this?

CHAPTER 35

Beware of modeling bad habits

One of my clients commented that she picked up a bad habit from her manager, which is checking her BlackBerry while she's talking to someone. She was embarrassed to talk about this, because she knows that it's rude. On the other hand, she rationalized the behavior by saying she unintentionally mimicked her manager.

This made me think about role models. When we purposefully model someone's behavior, we select the good characteristics. When we're not consciously thinking about it, however, it's easy to adopt bad characteristics.

Since my client talked about this, I've paid closer attention. Even the smallest things can be transmitted in a short time. For example, at the beginning of a meeting, one person was fidgeting with a pen, and by the end of the meeting, two others were doing it.

In another case, someone who is normally quite articulate started injecting a lot of "ums" into his speech, because someone else in the conversation was doing so.

None of these are earthshaking behaviors. But they're symptomatic of worse things you can unconsciously adopt. You can absorb bad moods or lousy morale even more quickly than you can start tapping a pen.

Leaders need to be keenly aware of how they appear to others, so learn to be acutely conscious of *how* and *what* you do, especially in front of others. Use this checklist as a guide:

- Am I focused or distracted?
- Have I chosen to maintain a neutral to positive attitude, regardless of what's happening in the environment?
- Am I aware of the behavior of those around me, and how I may be absorbing it?
- Do I want to be emotionally engaged in a conversation or be more objective and analytical?
- Does my current behavior reflect the person I want to portray?

The good news is that you can change bad habits. Observe yourself for a few days, and shift away from what doesn't work for you.

For reflection:

- Observe both the good and bad habits that you exhibit in front of your staff.
- Consciously eliminate the bad habits and replace them with ones that reflect a better role model.

CHAPTER 36

SHADES OF BLACK

Experienced managers routinely make decisions that are essentially black-and-white. But have you ever noticed that *how* you execute those decisions can make a difference in outcome?

I think of this as "shades of black," which is really about nuances. You know you're functioning within the realm of black, but which black is it?

Leaders deal with shades of black all of the time. For example:

- Your client is pressing you on a number of things—all of which need to be addressed—and you need to decide which to handle first.
- You have an employee who needs to improve in several different areas, and you decide which aspect needs to be tackled first for optimum results.

- Your board wants information that is easy to gather but time-consuming. Which of your already overloaded people should take on the assignment?

In each of these examples, you know what you need to do, but will you capture the nuances so you create the most impact?

In the first example, clearly you need to respond proactively since it's your client, but your decision about where to start will determine what will set the stage and have the most and best impact as you proceed.

You could tell your employee everything that needs improvement, but doing so could be demoralizing and frustrating. Your decision involves thinking through the ripple effect of what to address first.

Any of your staff can do the board project, but which person will add that extra touch that will go above and beyond the board's expectations?

We deal with shades of black all of the time. When you master this, you will be tuned into nuances of your environment in entirely different ways.

Your decisions aren't just about the black and white; they're about considering the dimensions that will lead to more spectacular results with your clients and your employees.

For reflection:

- How do you handle shades of black?
- Identify some benefits you will gain by mastering these nuances.

CHAPTER 37

CONNECT THE DOTS

Have you gone to a doctor lately? I think most people would agree that when it comes to diagnosing non-routine illnesses, the überspecialization of medicine makes it more difficult to grasp the "big picture." Even internists have a harder time because there are so many moving parts.

What do you do in these situations? Surely, you can't be expected to connect the dots!

Of course, no one supposes you will solve a medical mystery. I only use the medical example because so many people can relate to it.

But I think this is a much bigger theme. I see instances of it throughout the workplace. For example:

- People begin a new job, and it's up to them to figure out how to navigate through the firm's unique culture.
- Many employees don't know how their performance is judged.

- Career management is an afterthought of professional development, and if you try to figure it out on your own, you don't really know how to get from where you are now to where you want to go.
- When you start to pay attention to this, you'll notice variations on the theme. The bottom line is that one of the workplace skills that we need to cultivate is the ability to connect the dots.

The twenty-first-century version, however, adds the important complication of not knowing where some of the dots are. This means we need to make educated guesses of not only *where* they are but also *what* they are.

Here are two issues to ponder. First, what can you do to eliminate gaps in your organization, such as the ones mentioned above? It may be useful for you to look at your company with "alien eyes" to evaluate and improve such scenarios. (In fact, this could be a great team project.)

Second, what can you do to help your people develop a greater ability to connect the dots? They will be more equipped to provide superior solutions on the job when they cultivate this skill. Hint: try some combination of creative and systematic thinking (I know; they're opposites, but that's the point!).

For reflection:

- Identify how you can connect the dots in your organization.
- What type of outcome do you desire from doing this?

CHAPTER 38

WORKPLACE DRAMA

How often does your staff create distractions with an avalanche of finger-pointing and accusations? "He said this" and "She did that" and "I don't know anything about this" are expressions that you'll typically hear.

If you hear these types of phrases occasionally, it's normal and controllable. But if these expressions occur regularly over time, you may be a party to workplace drama.

It's up to the leader to cut off this behavior before it ramps up, because frequent incidences are bad for your organization's health. Often, the right hand doesn't know what the left is saying or doing; and that is where the problems begin.

When this goes unchecked, trust decreases, gossip increases, and, of course, productivity plummets. The cost of the lost productivity is huge, and over time, it takes a major toll.

It's important to realize that the subject of this workplace drama is often not what the bickering or finger-pointing is about. The outward conversation may be symptomatic of something deeper and potentially more damaging.

Good leaders know how to ask the right questions and get to the heart of the issue. After doing this, they may need to referee, mediate, or otherwise interfere to stop the drama. At times this can be painful, but it's much less painful than doing nothing.

If leaders are ignorant about internal strife, then they're not doing an important part of their job, which is to walk around and take the pulse and temperature of their staff. It's your job to do this; you're not supposed to stay in your office with the door closed and assume that everything is going well.

This is more than "management by walking around." It involves concentrated powers of observation and a willingness to discover and deal with something that may not be so pleasant.

Has drama crept into your company? If it's slipping into your culture, you know what you need to do.

For reflection:

- How can you determine if workplace drama is hiding in plain sight?
- What can you do to prevent it from starting?

CHAPTER 39

PERK UP YOUR COMPANY

A *Wall Street Journal* showcased the latest and greatest perks in start-up companies. Firm-wide social calendars, theme days, and living rooms (including a tree house) have sprouted, providing work environments that presumably keep these workers engaged.

This engagement strategy is created by and for the millennials. These new corporate cultures are as comfortable as old shoes and more akin to camp than conventional workplaces.

Of course, business cycles occur, and just as the perks that emerged during the tech euphoria of the '90s disappeared when that bubble burst, today's perks may have a limited life expectancy.

But that's almost irrelevant. The bigger issue is this: when employees believe these types of benefits are part of the job, they're no longer perks. They're the new *status quo*.

Why is this important to you? Well, for one thing, employee expectations will change. Young people leaving these perk-heavy firms may anticipate something comparable when they change jobs. They'll just assume you offer something similar to what they have come to expect.

One CEO recently complained to me, "Why do we have to have another pizza night?" Of course, he knows the answer. What he doesn't know is when such events morphed from occasions into traditions in his firm.

I'm not suggesting that you turn your organization into a playground but that you be mindful of what's happening elsewhere. And if you happen to be rolling your eyes as you read this, think of it this way: a little dose of fun might engage you more, too.

For reflection:

- What can you do to "perk up" your organization?
- Who can help you so that this doesn't drift into yet another item on your to-do list?

CHAPTER 40

Break down silos and build trust

Everyone knows leadership teams need to develop trust in order to work together effectively. In spite of this common knowledge, the development of silos—departments that operate independently rather than cooperatively—can present obstacles to developing this trust.

Leaders need to be mindful of this, because once the silos are established, it becomes much harder to eliminate them and work collaboratively. Self-interest becomes a substantial barrier to teamwork.

I've had numerous opportunities to facilitate trust building in companies where the silos seemed impenetrable, so I wanted to share a few ideas for developing trust (and preventing those silos from happening in the first place):

- Provide an opportunity for more personal interaction in your leadership team. Host breakfast or lunch periodically, so leaders get to know each other in a more informal environment.

- Allow room for mistakes, and make sure people learn from them. A culture of punishment detracts from trust building, while a learning environment enhances creativity.
- Ask for feedback, and listen to what people say. When you take action on someone's idea, others will feel encouraged to come up with even more ideas.
- Keep your word. If someone tells you something in confidence, don't "confidentially" discuss the matter with anyone.
- Give your people the opportunity to be who they are. A focus on strict corporate conformity can delay the trust-building process and deter authentic interaction.

Members of your leadership team don't have to become best friends. They do need to be role models, however, so that your organization functions smoothly and their own teams play well together in the sandbox.

For reflection:

- How can you build higher levels of trust in your organization?
- In what ways can you prevent silos from developing?

CHAPTER 41

THE POWER OF ASSOCIATION

Our colleagues influence our thoughts and behavior. Consider, for example, what it's like to be around people who are curious and explore new ideas as opposed to those who are content with the same old, same old.

All types of people surround us in the workplace. You know that people with negative attitudes can bring you down. But even people who have good attitudes but don't stretch their minds can harmful to our mental health.

This is subtle. Your coworkers might be nice people, but if they aren't interested in expanding their horizons, their stagnation may impact how you approach your own desire to expand and improve.

We are what we think about, and we are who we associate with.

Think about the people with whom you spend the most time. Do their ideas stimulate you? Do they ask questions that challenge your thinking? Do you feel a little more fired up as a result of being around them?

What do you think about, and with whom do you want to associate?

I'm not suggesting you shun your colleagues or move your office; rather, it's a gentle reminder about the power of association. Think about the attributes that you value, and associate with people who share your interests and aspirations.

I once learned a Bajan saying which nicely captures this sentiment, "Show me your company, and I'll tell you who you are."

For reflection:

- What do your personal associations say about who you are?
- How can you expand your horizons through new associations?

CHAPTER 42

ON-THE-JOB ENTITLEMENT

When organizations undergo change—whether it's growth or restructuring or new lines of business—it's easy to divert your attention from people issues. You can go into autopilot, assuming that people will do their jobs, and, frankly, you hope for the best while you focus on other priorities.

When left unchecked, however, you may find yourself with a disgruntled staff that feels overworked, underappreciated, and worst of all, entitled.

Entitled employees have ridiculous expectations, such as wanting more compensation "because they deserve it." They can also resist pitching in and doing tasks for the betterment and benefit of their team and the organization as a whole because "what's in it for them?"

One of my clients had a professional-level employee who was absent 42 percent of the time…because her car was broken…her foot was injured…her mother needed to go to the doctor…you get the idea.

If you have signs of this happening, you need to take action immediately. When attitudes of entitlement creep into your company, they can become cancerous and spread quickly, especially when you're not paying attention.

This is a complex topic, because entitled employees have different levels of performance. The decision is easy if someone is entitled and not doing his or her job. It's more complicated if the person does an excellent job but acts entitled.

If you try to change entitled attitudes and they still persist, it's probably time to make a change in personnel. These decisions aren't easy, but the bottom line is the bottom line. You can always train someone to do a job, but when it comes to an entitled attitude, all bets are off.

For reflection:

- How do you deal with entitlement?
- What do you do to change an environment of entitlement?

CHAPTER 43

MENTAL RETROFITTING

I'll bet that you *love* dealing with technology changes…
Even if you're a techie, you have to admit most people wrestle with technology changes, especially how to get up to speed with new procedures and processes. Leaders and workers at all levels struggle with this.

Of course, most employers provide some sort of training to ease the pain during software upgrades or technology transitions. More often than not, though, this training provides only the foundation. Then it's up to the worker to learn on the job.

I've had this experience with something as innocuous as getting a new smartphone. I learned the basics, but within a couple of days, I ran into obstacles. In one case, I accidentally locked the keyboard and didn't know how to unlock it!

But that's not even the problem.

The real challenge is that many of our employees aren't keeping up. Yes, they receive the training, and yes, they do their jobs, but their *minds* need to be retrofitted. How many of your people are so mired in the past that their attitudes are keeping them from advancing into the future?

Several of my clients deal with this issue regularly. In spite of enthusiastic and patient leadership, some of their workers resist the new ways and long for the old days. They are so terrified to go out of their comfort zone that at some point they become liabilities.

Are you doing the same thing? If your mind is locked in the past, you need to mentally retrofit, or not only will you hold yourself back, but you'll slow down those who work for you, too.

If you're comfortable keeping pace with technological changes, lend a hand or offer resources to those who are stuck.

The pace of technological change is only going to get faster, so this skill of mental retrofitting might well be a necessity for the future.

For reflection:

- Where do you need a mental retrofit?
- How can you bring your employees out of their comfort zone for the benefit of keeping pace with change?

CHAPTER 44

DECLARATION OF INTERDEPENDENCE

Many of my clients and friends rank "independence" as one of their most important personal values, so it's worthwhile to reflect on what independence means to you from a personal perspective.

To be independent is to not be controlled by others. Independence can mean a state of self-reliance and self-sufficiency. It can also mean a desire for freedom. These characterizations have slightly different meanings, which are subtle yet important to distinguish.

When I discuss why independence is important in leadership seminars, people raise these and other distinctions. What inevitably follows, though, is a discussion about the importance of *inter*dependence.

Leadership is enhanced by knowing when to be collegial, when to ask for help, and how to best collaborate with others. This is the essence of interdependence.

Some people are afraid that interdependence will detract from how others perceive them. On the contrary, knowing how and when to function interdependently is a quality that often separates top performers from the pack.

How does the concept of interdependence come to life for you? Everyone contributes something to the party, with the end result being much richer than one leader's efforts alone. The contributions of others enhance the whole.

Your colleagues *want* to contribute to the greater good. When people feel like they have meaningful roles, they are more engaged.

For reflection:

- How can you foster interdependence?
- What can you change about your personal leadership style to enable this goal?

CHAPTER 45

RISING ABOVE DISAPPOINTMENTS

We all deal with little victories and disappointments on a regular basis, but every once in a while, a biggie happens. It's easy to celebrate the big victories but more challenging to manage big disappointments.

This could be the expectation of receiving an important promotion, a new and better job, or an opportunity to break into a new client relationship. It doesn't matter what it is; if you had your heart set on it and it doesn't happen, it can feel like a setback.

Managers need to be aware when this happens to their employees and provide them with ways to overcome the letdown. Here are some ideas to share with them when this happens.

- Ask them to reflect on how they presented their credentials and experience. Could they have packaged themselves or the company differently?

- If there is a way to ask for direct feedback from the decision maker, suggest that they solicit it. Many decision makers are generally willing to share their opinions, so it's well worth following up when you can.
- Can they benefit from developing additional skills or experience so they're better prepared the next time? If so, suggest they take steps to acquire that new knowledge.
- Ask them (hindsight being twenty-twenty) whether this opportunity was all they thought it would be. After going through the experience, the promotion may not have been all it was cracked up to be, or the client opportunity may have been off base.

In any situation like this, help them flesh out what they learned from the experience so that they're better positioned and prepared the next time around.

And of course, like falling off of the proverbial bicycle, make sure they get up and try again soon.

For reflection:

- How do you help your people manage disappointments?
- How do you handle and bounce back from your own disappointments?

CHAPTER 46

LEARNING MOMENTS

Have you ever done something a little out of your comfort zone that seemed daunting before you did it? Of course you have! You also know, then, how great it feels when you blast through the fear and just do it. In fact, often you feel so good that it's hard to remember what made you nervous a few minutes earlier.

Lifelong learning is a value that is important to many leaders; in fact, many people learn aspects of their businesses while on the job. When you think about this, you'll observe that you have many opportunities to apply this concept with your employees.

When you introduce a new project or concept to one of your people, it triggers a number of things:

- The brain is stimulated differently as the "newness" of the idea creates additional neural pathways.
- It creates "positive stress" with a mix of emotions related to doing something new.

- It is an act of confidence that demonstrates your belief in your employee's ability.

My observation is these types of projects get waylaid because the manager thinks that he or she needs to be a subject-matter expert in the new project. That's a mistake. You don't have time to be an expert in everything, and you don't need to be an expert to facilitate, coach, or mentor the learning process of your people.

So, what have you held on the sidelines that could be turned into a productive opportunity to grow your business *and* your people? Give your people the chance to feel great by temporarily taking them out of their comfort zone.

For reflection:

- How can you sell the benefits of positive stress to your staff?
- Think about what it means if you're *not* a subject-matter expert in everything your people do.

CHAPTER 47

FROM JUDGER TO LEARNER

We spend considerable time judging so many different things: people, situations, and opinions, to name a few. When you find yourself in the judger mind-set, though, how receptive are you to new ideas? How open are you? How eager are you to expand your perspective?

Think of this as a continuum with "judger" on one end and "learner" on the other. The closer you are to the learner end of this scale, the more open you are. And the nearer you are to the judger end, the more closed you tend to be.

It's a great concept, because you can be entirely conscious about your mind-set at any moment. The best part is that when you find yourself slipping into judger, you can make the choice to shift into learner immediately.

When you're a learner, you're open to new ideas. You have greater curiosity. You want to explore.

Now, imagine what this would be like for the people who work for you. Our people take their cues from us, so this idea has unlimited possibilities.

To measure the impact of this concept, engage your team in a short exercise during a staff meeting. Divide your people into two groups, and make one group the judgers and the other the learners. Pick a topic and begin a dialogue based on the identified roles.

Everyone will benefit from this, and it will make the point in an engaged and entertaining way.

For reflection:

- How can you personally shift to becoming more of a learner?
- How does being a judger benefit you? How does it detract from your effectiveness?

CHAPTER 48

CREATIVE COMPETITIVENESS

In "The Creative Monopoly," the *New York Times* op-ed columnist David Brooks presented an interesting commentary on the potential conflict between competitiveness and creativity.

He observes that "the competitive spirit capitalism engenders can sometimes inhibit the creativity it requires." Creative people dart and weave in search of solutions. Traditional competitors, on the other hand, are so focused on beating the competition that they may miss other alternatives or opportunities.

The foundation for this dichotomy rests in the educational arena, where students are encouraged to strive for all As, rather than focus on their areas of greatest strength or interest. The corporate environment takes this a step farther: it frowns when someone appears to go "off point," which is exactly what creatives do best.

Of course, it's possible to create a balance between creativity and competition. You can develop this balance by being aware of the inherent conflicts and taking action to promote and support creative pursuits while not losing focus on the end goal.

Organizations that foster this balance will develop an edge. You will get the best of your people's creativity, which may lead to even better solutions than you originally envisioned.

When you encourage attributes such as independent thinking and resourcefulness, your people will respond by bringing out their best. Your organization benefits, so everyone wins.

For reflection:

- How do you manage the balance between creativity and competitiveness?
- How can you encourage better independent and critical thinking in your company?

CHAPTER 49

COLLABORATING IN TRANSITION

Have you ever moved into a new leadership role and panicked because the job seemed overwhelming? Since the workplace trend is to pile on more responsibilities with fewer resources, this can be daunting for someone moving into a new role.

Ideally, you'd have a chance to adjust to the new role in a paced and systematic manner, but today that is usually more fantasy than reality. Regrettably, transitions are increasingly unstructured and pose more questions than answers.

One of the patterns that occur during such transitions is that the new manager thinks that it's important to be the rugged individualist that served him or her well climbing the leadership ladder. Self-reliance is great, but not at the expense of an effective transition into a new role.

Don't be shy about reaching out for support from colleagues who may have insight and perspective that can help you. It's *not* a sign of weakness to ask questions and to learn the lay of the land from others who have been there, done that.

When you take a collaborative approach by reaching out to colleagues, it will expedite the move into the new role. Importantly, the best advice may come from a surprising source, so be open to what you may discover from anyone.

Another tip is to step outside of the day-to-day craziness in your work environment and take time to think and reflect. This can be as easy as taking a ten-minute break in Starbucks.

You may have heard of the concept of the "third place." These are locations outside of our home or workplace where we can be alone in the midst of others. A casual conversation with someone sitting near you may even trigger a thought that otherwise wouldn't have happened.

The bottom line is this: use the resources around you to help navigate through a leadership transition. It will shorten your learning curve and hopefully help you arrive at the more interesting parts of the job sooner than you expect.

For reflection:

- How can you decrease rugged individualism and become more collaborative?
- How can your experience benefit the next leader who joins your company?

CHAPTER 50

A LEADERSHIP QUANDARY

At one time or another, entrepreneurial leaders face the challenge of transitioning from "doing the doing" to leading their organizations. Many of my clients have passed through various stages of this transition, and frankly, it's not an easy one.

They just can't help themselves. They are passionate about their businesses yet wear blinders that they are the best people to accomplish the functional jobs that they're leaving behind.

They struggle with this leadership quandary. Intellectually, they need to let go, but emotionally they don't want to.

(By the way, this isn't a syndrome exclusive to owner/entrepreneurs. It's rampant in companies when top performers are promoted into management jobs and hold on to doing the doing rather than managing the doers.)

How do you break through this dilemma?

First, acknowledge the difference in roles and that yours is shifting to a new one that requires a different set of skills.

Second, identify the competencies that are essential to success in the leadership role versus the role of the doer. Objectively assess where you have strengths and areas for improvement.

Next, make the commitment to shift into your leadership role. This is a mind-set shift, and don't expect it to happen overnight. It's easy to slip back into the mind-set of the doer, especially if you're really good at it.

Instead, focus on what will help you move ahead purposefully as the leader. If you need some help, hire a coach or seek out a mentor who can guide you.

Even though this transition may seem difficult at first, it will be well worth it when you're aligned with moving ahead as a leader. In fact, it just might be the differentiator between business success and stagnation.

For reflection:

- How can you commit to stop "doing the doing" so that you can be more successful in your leadership role?
- What skills do you need to develop in order to help that process?

CHAPTER 51

CHANGING ROLES

Several clients are undergoing shifts in their roles. Some are changing to new roles internally, while others are exiting to new opportunities. Regardless of the situation, leaders need to be aware of the reverberations when announcing such a change.

This may not seem like a big deal, but if the outcome is like that unexpected blast of summer heat, it's not likely to be the smooth transition you hope for. As a leader, be prepared and proactive when these changes occur.

Be transparent. Tell the person *why* the change in role is happening and why you made this particular decision. He or she will appreciate your clarity but will resent it if you're elusive and not forthcoming.

Rally the team. If the person works with a team, make sure you take time to explain the change to them. They'll want to know how it affects them, and some will want to know if change is on the horizon for them as well.

Manage perceptions. This is especially important if others in the organization perceive the change of role as neutral or negative, and the actual change is positive.

Offer help. The person in transition can always benefit from some assistance. When you lead the way by offering resources, it will make a positive impression.

Say thank you. Remember to acknowledge the work of the person whose role is changing. This will help bring closure.

We usually think of organizational change in terms of larger-scale changes. In reality, changing one role can have a meaningful impact on team dynamics.

When you handle this proactively and with some sensitivity, the results will be more effective. In fact, it will seem more like a gradual change of season than a dramatic change in temperature.

For reflection:

- How can you more effectively manage role changes in your company?
- How can you help mentor a person undergoing such a change?

CHAPTER 52

ACKNOWLEDGING MILESTONES

G oing, going, gone!
Many companies operate at warp speed these days. Increasingly, fewer people are tasked with more robust workloads, and management expectations are higher than ever.

Sound familiar?

One of the fallouts of this dynamic is that people attain goals but move on to the next ones without regard to what they just achieved. This is a mistake. Recognizing achievements is an important action that you should not bypass.

Acknowledgment of professional milestones is an important workplace ritual. It's a way to bring closure to specific accomplishments and to salute those who were instrumental in doing the work.

In other cases, it might be appropriate to conduct a debriefing to highlight what was done well and consider how other aspects of the project could be done more effectively in the future.

When you take time to do this, your staff will react positively because they appreciate the recognition and may be motivated to do an even better job the next time.

If you choose to ignore milestones, not only are you shortchanging your staff; you're inadvertently diminishing the importance or value of the initiative that you completed. Over time, you may convey a message (intentionally or not) that the work itself isn't so important.

Everyone is busy. That said, you'll get a lot of mileage when you pause to acknowledge organizational milestones. And as an unintended benefit, this recognition might even pump up your people as they launch the next initiative.

For reflection:

- How can you "ritualize" the important milestones in your company?
- What are the benefits in doing so?

Acknowledgements

Many people helped to bring this project to fruition, and I am grateful for their contributions.

Emily Soccorsey reviewed the manuscript and provided editorial guidance. Along with her business partner, Justin Foster, they provided keen insights and perspective.

Darlene Belanger combed through hundreds of *Executive Insight Tip of the Week* issues to select the ones that became chapters in this book. Angelina Briggs created and designed the cover. Stephanie Cella supported content development.

Leigh Talmage provided ongoing wise counsel during the process, as she has for many projects over the many years we've known each other.

—*LMA*

About the Author

Dr. Lisa M. Aldisert is an internationally recognized business advisor, trend expert, speaker, and author. She is president of Pharos Alliance Inc., an executive advisory firm specializing in strategic planning, organizational and leadership development for entrepreneurial organizations.

Based in New York City, Lisa has over 35 years of experience, offering clients financial acumen, trend analysis, and leadership insight. She spent 16 years in the banking industry in multinational banking and corporate finance prior to starting her business.

Her blend of experience working with corporate conglomerates, privately held businesses operated by entrepreneurs, and being a business owner herself makes her a unique advisor. She strengthens connections between CEOs and their management teams, analyzes and enhances organizational dynamics, and assesses areas to improve systems and procedures.

When not working with clients, Lisa enjoys opportunities to present on strategic business topics. With a delivery style described as "insightful," "compelling," and "thoroughly enjoyable," she provides a unique perspective on leadership, women in business, entrepreneural and family-owned enterprises, and workplace trends.

Lisa is also the author of *Valuing People: How Human Capital Can Be Your Strongest Asset* (Dearborn) and is the co-author of *The Small Business Money Guide: How to Get It, Use It, Keep It* (Wiley). She is a contributing columnist for business and professional periodicals.

For more information, please feel
free to visit www.lisaaldisert.com
and stay connected by signing up for the
e-zine that inspired this book.
Feel free to follow Lisa at @LisaAldisert.

41302738R00067

Made in the USA
Middletown, DE
08 March 2017